To

Dearest Ileana on your 22nd
Birthday. when ~~~~~~~~ you
K-day, I Re~~~~~~~ you
were born, since then you have
brought so much, Joy, happiness
& love to my life.

Have a wonderful Birthday.
love you lots.

Mum ♡

Every
DAUGHTER
should have
a book
like this...

Other Titles in This Series:

Every Mom Should Have a Book like This
Filled with Love and Appreciation

Every Sister Should Have a Book like This
to Let Her Know What a Blessing She Is

Every Son Should Have a Book like This
Filled with Wishes, Love, and
Encouragement

Copyright © 2008 by Blue Mountain Arts, Inc.

We wish to thank Susan Polis Schutz for permission to reprint the following poem that appears in this publication: "You can depend on my support...." Copyright © 1986 by Stephen Schutz and Susan Polis Schutz. All rights reserved.

No part of this publication may be reproduced, stored in a retrieval system or transmitted in any form or by any means, electronic, mechanical, photocopying, recording or otherwise, without the written permission of the publisher.

All writings are by Douglas Pagels except as noted.

Library of Congress Control Number: 2007937493
ISBN: 978-1-59842-195-8

◪ and Blue Mountain Press are registered in U.S. Patent and Trademark Office. Certain trademarks are used under license.

Acknowledgments appear on page 72.

Printed in China.
First Printing: 2008
✹ This book is printed on recycled paper.

This book is printed on fine quality, laid embossed, 80 lb. paper. This paper has been specially produced to be acid free (neutral pH) and contains no groundwood or unbleached pulp. It conforms with the requirements of the American National Standards Institute, Inc., so as to ensure that this book will last and be enjoyed by future generations.

Blue Mountain Arts, Inc.

P.O. Box 4549, Boulder, Colorado 80306

Every

DAUGHTER

should have
a book
like this

to remind
her how
wonderful she is

Douglas Pagels

Blue Mountain Press™
Boulder, Colorado

Contents

Whenever I see you... 6

I wish I could find the words... 8

Through all the best moments... 10

Quote by Winston Groom 11

Daughter, Thanks for All the Smiles You've Given Me 12

Quote by Susan Polis Schutz 14

Sometimes we need reminders in our lives... 15

A Little Note with a Lot of Love 16

Having someplace to go is home 19

May You Remember... 20

Quote by Goldie Hawn 22

I want you to know that I would gladly drop whatever... .. 23

As the Years Go By 24

Old Proverb 27

A Little Prayer I'd Love to Share with You 28

Quote by Kristine Van Raden 30

If Anyone Knows... It's Me 31

To My Amazing, Remarkable Daughter 32

Quote by Carol Lynn Pearson 35

Something for My Beautiful Daughter to Remember
    Forever 36

Quote by Mary Matalin 38

These Are the Gifts I'll Always Wish for You 39

May you find happiness in every direction... 40

It would bring me more joy than I can say... 42

Quote by Al Roker 43

When It's Time to Fly 44

Quote by Margaret Wise Brown 46

Once upon a Time 47

Quote by Charles Dickens 51

A Few Words from the Heart 52

Life is not measured by... 54

You are so deserving of every good thing... 55

If there is ever a time when I can help in any way... 56

I am so blessed by the thousands... 58

Quote by James Russell Lowell 59

Remember... I'll always love you 60

Quote by Judy Swank 62

I'd like to share this thought with you... 63

May You Always Have an Angel by Your Side 64

Daughter, do you know what my favorite things... 66

Quote by Molly Davis 67

My favorite things are the birthdays... 68

Quote by Douglas Pagels 70

Until then, let me close by just saying... 71

Acknowledgments 72

Remember What This Says...

Whenever I see you, my beautiful daughter, I know I am looking at the smiling face of one of the most wonderful people I will ever have the privilege of knowing...

6

Whenever I am reminded of you, I find
so many hopes and memories in my heart.
Those thoughts and remembrances...
they're my favorite treasures, and nothing
warms my heart like they do.

Whenever I think of you, I think of how
precious you've always been and how
close I hope we'll always be.

If I could be given any gift imaginable,
one that would make me happy beyond
words, make me feel truly blessed, and
make my days just shine...

The gift I'd choose... would be you.

Each and every time.

I wish I could find the words to tell you how great it is to be the parent of a daughter like you.

The perfect words would tell you how proud I am of all you've done and everything you've become.

The ideal words would say what a joy it was to watch you grow up and what an amazing and rewarding and loving experience it continues to be.

Every time I see you, I know that I am looking at as beautiful a present as anyone has ever been given.

And I know that I could have hoped and prayed and dreamed all my life... and I could have wished on a million stars.

But I couldn't have been blessed with anyone more wonderful... than the daughter that you are.

Through all the best moments of life, from holding you in my arms when you were little to holding you in my heart every moment, I have always felt like I was the luckiest parent in the world.

One of the nicest things that could happen to anyone... happened to me. I've been able to not only raise an exquisite daughter, but also to watch a miracle in the making.

*And that lovely miracle
...is you.*

Remember What Winston Said...

A dozen of our friends were in the waiting room outside, and I heard the cheer go up all the way down the hall as soon as somebody announced, "It's a girl!"

...The years since have passed so quickly, life seems to have become like one of those time-lapse pictures of a growing flower.

— Winston Groom

Daughter, Thanks for All the Smiles You've Given Me

I want you to know how much you're treasured and celebrated and quietly thanked.

I want you to feel really good... about who you are. About all the great things you do! I want you to appreciate your uniqueness. Acknowledge your talents and abilities. Realize what a beautiful soul you have. Understand the wonder within.

*You make so much sun shine
through, and you inspire so much
joy in the lives of everyone who
is lucky enough to know you.*

*You are a very special person,
giving so many people a reason
to smile. You deserve to receive
the best in return, and one of
my heart's favorite hopes is that
the happiness you give away will
come back to warm you each
and every day of your life.*

Remember What
Susan Said...

*You can depend on
my support, guidance
friendship and love
every minute of every day*

— *Susan Polis Schutz*

Sometimes we need reminders in our lives of how much people care. If you ever get that feeling, I want you to remember this...

I love you, Daughter.

Beyond words that can even begin to tell you how much, I hold you and your happiness within my heart each day. I am so proud of you and so thankful to the years that have given me so much to be thankful for.

If I were given a chance to be anything I wanted to become, there's nothing I would rather be... than your parent.

And there is no one I would rather have ...as my daughter.

A Little Note with a Lot of Love

You are such a precious, extraordinary person. It's just amazing to see the things you've grown up to be. You impress me so much with all the things you've learned, all the things you care about, and all the things you understand.

You know that it's all about making the most of your life and of the time you have been given. About doing the best you can do — and letting go of the things that are beyond your control.

It's about believing in tomorrow and stretching your wings. Embracing your blessings and appreciating all the sweet memories you have made. It's about reaching for your stars, brightening your days, and filling your heart in a thousand ways.

It's about lifting up others, sharing the load, and continuing down the path on the way to making things better than they were before. It's about taking the next step into whatever lies ahead...

It's about finding out that you'll never need to feel alone and that your family, your faith, your hopes, and your dreams will be with you forever.

And it's about remembering, no matter what, that you'll always be the most welcomed and wonderful part of... a special place called home.

Remember What This Says...

Having someplace to go
   is home.
Having someone to love
   is family.
Having both
   is a blessing.

— *Anonymous*

May You Remember...

Daughter, in your happiest and most exciting moments, my heart will celebrate and smile beside you.

In your lowest lows, my love will be there to keep you warm, to give you strength, and to remind you that your sunshine is sure to come again.

In your moments of accomplishment, I will be filled so full of pride that I may have a hard time keeping the feeling inside of me.

*In your moments of disappointment, I will
be a shoulder to cry on, a hand to hold,
and a love that will gently enfold you
until everything's okay.*

*In your gray days, I will help you search,
one by one, for the colors of the rainbow.*

Remember What Goldie Said...

Daughters never really leave their mothers, and thank God for that. I couldn't imagine my life without her to share it with.

— Goldie Hawn

I want you to know that I would gladly drop whatever I'm doing, at any time of the day, just to have a chance to give you a hug, to say how much I care, and to share a few precious moments with you.

Right this very minute, I'd love nothing more than to be with you, looking at the smiling face of someone who has inspired so many smiles in my life.

I think of you all the time.

And even when we're not together, I take comfort in knowing that the caring and closeness between us will never change and that you'll always be in my heart.

As the Years Go By

I remember how I used to tuck you in at night. One of the sweetest jobs in the universe is giving a kiss and a hug and saying how much "I love you" to a sleepy child who thinks that "one more story" might be just about right. I remember weekends and pushing you in the swing and watching you reach for the sun and the moon and every star in the sky.

As time passed so quickly, and as you grew, I remember how you couldn't wait to show me the project or the picture of the day as soon as I'd see you after school. Even though your backpack was almost as big as you were, you never had any problem carrying all your things... and all my dreams for you... on those strong shoulders of yours.

I remember all the times I worried about you being gone too long from my sight. I remember the sweet feeling of seeing you again, even if it had only been a few hours since we'd been apart.

I remember thinking at least a million times what a joy you are to me and wondering how anyone could love someone as much as I love you.

The precious feeling remains with me right up to this very day. I am simply amazed at how the seasons have flown by and at how you have grown up so quickly... right before my eyes...

*When I look at you, I see someone
I cherish. I see someone I love with
every smile, every hope, every prayer,
and every treasured memory within
me. When I look at you, I see someone
who has so many paths yet to walk,
opportunities to explore, and stars to
keep on reaching for.*

*As the years go by, my hopes will travel
beside you on all your journeys. My
heart will still wish you sweet dreams at
night, and you will be a joy to me... all
your life.*

Remember How the Proverb Goes...

Parents hold their children's hands for a while... and their hearts forever.

— Old Proverb

A Little Prayer
I'd Love to Share
with You

*I want your life to be
    such a wonderful one.
I wish you peace. Deep within
    your soul.
Joyfulness. In the promise of
    each new day.
Stars. To reach for. Dreams.
    To come true.
Memories. More beautiful
    than words can say.*

*I wish you friends. Close at heart,
    even over the miles.
Loved ones. The best treasures
    we're blessed with.*

Present moments. To live in,
    one day at a time.
Serenity. With its wisdom.
    Courage. With its strength.
New beginnings. To give life a
    chance to really shine.

I wish you understanding. Of how
    special you really are.
A journey. Safe from the storms
    and warmed by the sun.
A path. To wonderful things.
An invitation. To the abundance
    life brings.
And an angel watching over.
    For all the days to come.

Remember What Kristine Said...

There is a part of me that wants to stop the clock right now. I want to keep you safe and protect you. I want to tuck you in night after night.

But I know that I cannot protect you, just like my mother knew, and hers, and hers. What I must continue to do instead is to teach you, guide you, honor you, and respect you....

I'll love you eternally.

— *Kristine Van Raden*

If Anyone Knows...
It's Me

Until you came along, I never would have imagined the joy I'd come to know. Until I was given the privilege of watching you grow into the unique, one-of-a-kind wonder that you are, I never could have imagined the depth of pride I'd feel inside.

If anyone has learned how much love a heart can hold, it's me. I'm so thankful that you're my daughter, and I'm so lucky that you're in my life.

To My Amazing, Remarkable Daughter

Everywhere you journey in life, you will go with my love by your side.

Forever it will be with you. Truly, joyfully, and more meant to be than words could ever say. You are the joy of my life, the source of my dearest memories, the inspiration for my fondest wishes, and you are the sweetest present life could ever give to anyone.

I love you so much. I want you to remember that... every single day. And I want you to know that these are things I'll always hope and pray...

That the world will treat you fairly. That people will appreciate the one-in-a-million person you are. That you will be safe and smart and sure to make good choices on your journey through life.

That a wealth of opportunities will come your way. That your blessings will be many, your troubles will be few, and that life will be very generous in giving you all the happiness and success you deserve...

You're not just a fantastic daughter. You're a tremendous, rare, and extraordinary person. All the different facets of your life — the ones you reveal to the rest of the world, and the ones known only to those you're close to — are so impressive. And as people look even deeper, I know they can't help but see how intrinsically beautiful you are.

I'll always love you with all my heart. And I couldn't be more proud of you... if I tried.

Remember What Carol Said...

"*Mother, if I did not grow to be just like you, are you disappointed?*"

The mother looked up....

"*Oh, no,*" *she said.* "*You are* you, *and you are better than I ever dreamed.*"

— Carol Lynn Pearson

Something for My Beautiful Daughter to Remember Forever

Has anyone told you lately what an exquisite person you are?

I hope so! I hope you've been told dozens of times... because you are simply amazing. And just in case you haven't heard those words in a while, I want you to hear them now. You deserve to know that...

*It takes someone special to do
what you do. It takes someone
rare and remarkable to make
the lives of everyone around
them nicer, brighter, and more
beautiful. It takes someone who
has a big heart and a caring soul.
It takes someone who's living
proof of how precious a person
can be.*

It takes someone... just like you.

Remember What Mary Said...

I pray every day that I can be your best mom for all time. Someone you can lean on for today's stubbed toe and tomorrow's bruised ego. Someone who can make sure that that laugh-out-loud glee that came with your first extraordinary, training-wheel-free, two-wheeler experience is there for all your life experiences to come.

— Mary Matalin

These Are the Gifts
I'll Always Wish for You

Happiness. Deep down within.
Serenity. With each sunrise.
Success. In each facet of your life.
Close and caring friends.
Love. That never ends.

Special memories. Of all the yesterdays.
A bright today. With much to
    be thankful for.
A path. That leads to beautiful tomorrows.

Dreams. That do their best to come true.
And appreciation. Of all the wonderful
    things about you.

May you find happiness in every direction your paths take you. May you never lose that sense of wonder you have always had, and may you hold on to the sense of humor you use to brighten the lives of everyone who knows you. May you go beyond the ordinary steps and discover extraordinary results. May you keep on trying to reach for your stars, and may you never forget how wonderful you are...

May you always be patient with the problems of life, and know that any clouds will eventually give way to the sunlight of your most hoped-for days. May you be rewarded with the type of friendships that get better and better — and the kind of love that blesses your life forever.

It would bring me more joy than I can say if you would never forget — not even for a single day — how wonderful you are... in my eyes and in my heart.

I'm so often at a loss to find the words to tell you how much you mean to me. In my imagination, I compare you with things like the sunshine in my mornings, the most beautiful flowers in the fields, and the happiness I feel on the best days of all.

Remember What Al Said...

She is anything
anyone
could ever want
in a daughter.

— Al Roker

When It's Time to Fly

There are so many new horizons ahead. In the blink of an eye, daughters are off to college, off to jobs, and eventually on to setting up their own homes and tending to their families and future lives. It's a time when parents hope and pray that all the values and lessons they tried to instill will help to light the way for the journey ahead.

And I am no exception: I want great things for you, too... and I have an enormous amount of faith in your ability to make your life a happy one.

*You take with you, everywhere you go,
a supply of confidence, common sense,
ability, determination, understanding,
wisdom, and so many attributes that
just sparkle inside you. You know how
to make the right choices, and I know
that you will.*

*But of all the things you take with you,
you should know that you also leave
something behind. Some people call it
an "empty nest," but in its own special
way, there's nothing empty about it. It
will always be abundantly filled with
wishes, support, hugs and hopes, an
open line of communication, a close
and caring bond, a sense of belonging,
and a strong and constant love.*

Remember What
Margaret Said...

*If you become a bird
and fly away from me...
I will be a tree
that you come home to.*

— Margaret Wise Brown

Once upon a Time

These days, the things that people read are sometimes in books, but are just as likely to be in magazines and on computer screens. But once upon a time, you and I spent so many perfect moments curled up together reading words just like those of Margaret Wise Brown's. We filled our home with those timeless books, and those stories warmed our hearts. When you were little, it was a very big thing to me to have that special kind of togetherness blessing our lives...

As the years have passed, I find that it's not just birds that fly... time does, too. And now the things I read aren't about runaway bunnies or saying "good night" to the moon. And I haven't seen a favorite bear there, pretending to be a rain cloud, when I go to turn the page. There used to be genies, hungry caterpillars, and wild things whisking our imaginations away, but these days our world is filled with so many different things.

The stories of our lives in the present day have pages, too. If we could read them now, they'd probably sound pretty sedate to some people, but they've been a grand adventure to me. I hope you'll feel the same way, every day, about your life.

As the pages fill up, I hope your life story takes you every special place you've ever dreamed of.

Just remember, Daughter, no matter where you go anytime you "fly away," there will always be a place that you can come home to...

No matter how long any journey
turns out to be, I know that you will
never forget which path to take...
to come home to me. I will always
be here with open arms, incredibly
thankful for our closeness and our
caring. And whether we're chatting
while we're stirring up something
in the kitchen, taking a long walk
with a lot of catching-up to do,
or just relaxing on the porch on
a summer's day that's still years
away, I'll always look forward to
having you share each one of your
stories... with me.

Remember What Charles Said...

*I celebrate... the day
that gave me
such a dear
and good daughter
as you.*

— *Charles Dickens*

A Few Words from the Heart

There is never a day that goes by without my thinking of what a beautiful blessing you are to my life. God must have been smiling down on me... when you came into the world. And I promise you this: it would be a far less fantastic, rewarding, and remarkable place... without you.

I am so enormously proud of you! I love you beyond all words that I will ever be able to say, and I will love you every moment.

There are gifts that are far above priceless. There are memories that are made of pure love. There are special miracles that really do come true.

And all my life, you will always be... a wonderful gift, a treasure of memories, and an amazing miracle... to me.

Remember What This Says...

Life is not measured by the number of breaths we take, but by the moments that take our breath away.

— *Anonymous*

You are so deserving of every good thing that can come your way. And I want you to know, if I could have a wish come true, I'd wish for every day of your life to be blessed with some special gift that warms your heart, some gentle smile that touches your soul, and so many things that simply take your breath away.

If there is ever a time when I can help in any way, with anything, I want you to know, my daughter, that you can turn to me.

It doesn't matter what it is... when it is... or where the two of us may be. What does matter to me is your well-being, your highest hopes, and your sweetest dreams.

I want that big, beautiful heart of yours to be filled with as much happiness as it can hold.

*I want the world to be so good
to you! I want it to give you an
abundance of love and warmth and
wonder... because that's exactly
what you deserve to receive.*

*So please remember this: you can
always count on me to be here for
you, cheering you up, cheering you
on, and just being there to love
you and to listen and to gently
understand.*

I am so blessed by the thousands of smiles we have shared, by the memories we have made, and by the way you will always be such a precious part of everything that home and love and family... will ever mean to me.

Remember What James Said...

Dearest daughter...
to you I send
the biggest kiss
that ever was.

— James Russell Lowell

Remember... I'll always love you. Remember... as you hold this in your hands and read these words, I'll hold you in a very precious place in my heart — as long as there are stars in the sky.

Remember — if I could — I would give you the moon and the sun in return for all the smiles and memories you've given me.

*And remember when I say "I love you,"
I want you to know what those words
really mean. "I love you" means that
you're the most wonderful daughter
there could ever be. It means that you
have made me more proud of you than
you could even begin to imagine. And
it means that I will never let a day
go by without feeling blessed by the
giving... of a gift like you.*

Remember What Judy Said...

I bless the day she came to me...
My little girl with the big brown eyes.
Through the years
she made me laugh so hard I cried.
She shared her dreams.
She shared her heart.
We shared the risks.
We share our love.
And she taught me courage
to find my way.
What beautiful, joyful moments we have had —
me and my little girl with the big brown eyes.

— Judy Swank

I'd like to share this thought
with you, to tell you that
  you mean the world to me.

Think of something you couldn't
  live without
  ...and multiply it by a hundred.
Think of what happiness means to you
  ...and add it to the feeling you get
    on the best days you've ever had.

Add up all your best feelings
and take away all the rest...
  and what you're left with is
    exactly how I feel about you.

You matter more to me than you can
  imagine and much more than I'll ever
    be able to explain.

May You Always Have an Angel by Your Side

May you always have an angel by your side • Watching out for you in all the things you do • Reminding you to keep believing in brighter days • Finding ways for your wishes and dreams to come true • Giving you hope that is as certain as the sun • Giving you the strength of serenity as your guide • May you always have love and comfort and courage •

May you always have an angel by your side • Someone there to catch you if you fall •

Encouraging your dreams • *Inspiring your happiness* • *Holding your hand and helping you through it all* • *In all our days, our lives are always changing* • *Tears come along as well as smiles* • *Along the roads you travel, may the miles be a thousand times more lovely than lonely* •

May they give you gifts that never, ever end: someone wonderful to love and a dear friend in whom you can confide • *May you have rainbows after every storm* • *May you have hopes to keep you safe and warm* •

• *And may you always have an angel by your side* •

Daughter, do you know what my favorite things in the whole world are?

They all seem to start with having you as such a precious part of my life.

It's listening to a voice that has changed from first words and the littlest sighs to words that now share the deepest feelings and the strongest trust. It's the memories made — shaped through the days and captured on every sunlit path we were given the grace... of walking together.

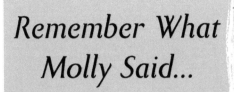

Remember What Molly Said...

Know that I am your greatest ally and fan. I will continue to applaud at your victories and walk with you through trials and mistakes....

I'll love you forever.

— Molly Davis

My favorite things are the birthdays, the holidays, the special days. It's knowing that you are reason enough to celebrate every day. It's cherishing the way our lives entwine. It's the listening that always leads to more closeness.

It's learning that nothing could ever be more valuable than our companionship and the constant bond that endears us to each other. It's me, watching from the sidelines, quietly bursting with pride, seeing the process of a beautiful flower unfolding before my eyes.

Daughter, the smiles you give me are such magnificent gifts. And I just can't help but think: someone else can win the lottery... and get all the prizes waiting to be won. Others can take their exotic travels, buy their mansions, and spend their entire lives adding to their worth.

I'm perfectly content to just close my eyes and to lovingly realize that, thanks to you...

I feel like the luckiest person on earth.

And Remember What I Said...

You've always known that you are my world.

And I hope this book has been able to tell you some of the reasons why. A few of the thoughts are things you are hearing for the first time. Others are things I've tried to say (in my own special way) and share with you all your life. And there are other thoughts that you and I will share in days ahead, when all the right words and the perfect moments come along.

— Douglas Pagels

Until then, let me close by just saying...

*Thank you. What an honor it has been.
Watching such a beautiful person
blossom. Someone I admire and adore
with all my heart. Thank you for
enriching my life beyond belief. Thank
you for the grace and the goodness, the
hopes, the memories, and the happiness.
Thank you for bringing so many
priceless gifts to me.*

I love you so much.